Canada

SEAN DOLAN

Raintree

www.raintreepublishers.co.uk
Visit our website to find out more information about Raintree books.

To order:
☎ Phone 44 (0) 1865 888112
🖹 Send a fax to 44 (0) 1865 314091
🖳 Visit the Raintree Bookshop at **www.raintreepublishers.co.uk** to browse our catalogue and order online.

First published in Great Britain by Raintree Publishers, Halley Court, Jordan Hill, Oxford, OX2 8EJ, part of Harcourt Education.
Raintree is a registered trademark of Harcourt Education Ltd.

© Harcourt Education Ltd 2003
First published in paperback 2004
The moral right of the proprieter has been asserted.

Editorial: Sally Knowles
Cover Design: Peter Bailey and Michelle Lisseter
Production: Jonathan Smith

Printed and bound in China and Hong Kong by South China Printing Company

ISBN 1 844 21311 0 (hardback)
07 06 05 04 03
10 9 8 7 6 5 4 3 2 1

ISBN 1 844 21325 0 (paperback)
08 07 06 05 04
10 9 8 7 6 5 4 3 2 1

British Library Cataloguing in Publication Data
Dolan, Sean
Canada. - (World tour)
971
A full catalogue for this book is available from the British Library

Acknowledgements
The publishers would like to thank the following for permission to reproduce photographs:
p. **1b** ©Thompson Martin/Spectrum Stock; p. **3a** ©Spectrum Stock; p. **5a** ©Bryan andCherry Alexander; p. **7** ©Spectrum Stock; p.**8** ©Bill Banaszewski/Visuals Unlimited;
p. **13a** ©Hubert Stadler/CORBIS; p. **13b** ©Thomas Kitchin/Tom Stack Associates; p. **15a** ©Steve Cohen/Houserstock; p. **15b** ©Joe Bensen/Stock Boston; p. **19** ©Ottmar Bierwagen Photo Inc./ Spectrum Stock; p. **21a** ©Connie Colaman/Getty Images; p. **21b** ©Dave G. Houser/Houserstock; p. **23** ©T. Kitchen/ Tom Stack & Associates; p. **27a** ©Mark Gibson; p. **27b** ©Kim Stallknecht/Spectrum Stock; p. **28** ©Annie Griffiths Belt/CORBIS; p. **29** ©Fred Chartrand/AP/Wide World; p. **31a** ©Jurgen Vogt/Getty Images; p. **31b** ©Robert B. McGouey/Spectrum Stock; p. **33** ©Dave G. Houser/Houserstock; p. **34** ©Bill Boch/ Foodpix; p. **35** ©Winston Fraser; p. **37** ©Galen Rowell/CORBIS; p. **38** ©Lowell Georgia/CORBIS; p. **39** ©Grise Ford/ SuperStock; p. **40** ©Lionel Delevingne/ Stock Boston; p. **41** ©Frank Scott/Spectrum Stock; p. **43b** ©Jean AEF.Duboisberranger/ Getty Images; p. **44a,b** ©Mitchell Gerber/ CORBIS; p. **44c** ©Reuters newMedia Inc./ CORBIS;

Additional photography by Comstock, Corbis Royalty Free and Getty Royalty Free PhotoDisc and Steck-Vaughn Collection.

Cover photography: Background: Getty Images/Taxi/Stan Osolinki. Foreground: Corbis/Gunter Marx Photography

Every effort has been made to contact copyright holders of any material reproduced in this book. Any omissions will be rectified in subsequent printing if notice is given to the publishers.

Contents

Welcome to Canada

Canada is on of the countries that make up the continent of North America. It is a wonderful country, famous for its national parks and lively cities. There is something for everyone to enjoy in the world's second-largest country. Canada has breathtaking natural beauty, friendly people, grand cities and an unusual history.

Some tips to get you started

• Use the table of contents

Do you already know what you are looking for? Perhaps you just want to know what topics this book will cover. The contents page tells you which topics you will read about and where they are found in the book.

• Look at the pictures

This book has lots of great photos. Flip through and look at the pictures you like best. They will give you an idea of what the book is all about. Read the captions to learn even more about the photos.

• Use the glossary

As you read this book, you may notice that some words appear in **bold** print. Look up bold words in the glossary in the back of the book. The glossary will help you learn what they mean.

▲ A GRAND MIDNIGHT LIGHT SHOW
The Aurora Borealis, also called
the Northern Lights, are seen in
the night sky over Manitoba,
Canada. Particles in the air cause
this colourful display.

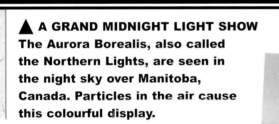

POLAR BEAR ▶
A large part of Canada is too
cold for people to live in, but is
just right for animals like this
polar bear. His thick fur and a
fatty layer of blubber under his
skin help keep him warm.

Canada's past

Canada's history is fascinating. The story of Canada's Native American nations and how the country has changed since the first Europeans settlers arrived there, explains the mixture of cultures and peoples that make up Canada today.

Ancient history

The first people arrived in Canada between 20,000 and 35,000 years ago, at the end of the last **Ice Age**. They developed into many different Native American peoples who settled across the **continent** and eventually developed into twelve different language groups.

From the 900s onwards, Viking sailors from Scandinavia reached Newfoundland, in eastern Canada, and many of them stayed for a while, but their small **settlements** did not last long.

Permanent European settlement of Canada did not take place until the sixteenth and seventeenth centuries. In the 1530s, the French sailor Jacques Cartier explored the Gulf of St Lawrence and the St Lawrence River. He became the first European to visit these sites, which were important Native American trading centres. Later, these same places became the Canadian cities of Québec and Montréal.

Cartier's discovery led France to claim and settle Canada. A Frenchman called Samuel de Champlain **founded** a settlement at Québec. He explored the land to the west, as far as the Great Lakes and Hudson **Bay**.

Empire of furs

Before long, French fur traders were using Canada's rivers and lakes to explore the west. Canada's forests were home to many animals with thick fur. These animals were caught and killed by trappers and the fur sold for lots of money. The coat of the beaver, in particular, was worth an enormous amount of money in Europe. People made large fortunes working in the Canadian fur trade. When the French fur traders came, the Catholic **missionaries** came too. They travelled far into the Canadian wilderness to convert the native peoples to Catholicism, a form of the Christian religion.

Canada's wealth from furs drew the attention of the British. British fur traders soon moved to Hudson Bay, to the north and west of the French settlements. In the 1700s, a struggle began between France and Great Britain for North American territory. This included land in what later became the USA.

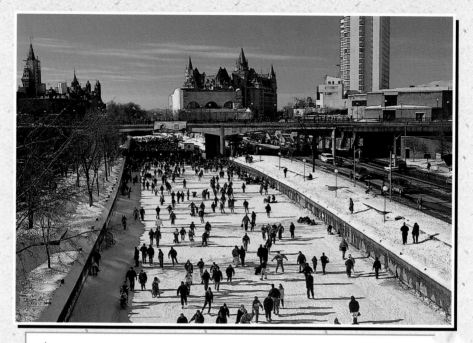

▲ **WINTER IN OTTAWA**
Ice skating on the Rideau Canal in Canada's capital city is fun during the Winterlude Festival. This skating rink is the longest in the world.

This struggle led to war between the French and British from 1754 to 1763. This is known as the French and Indian War because the French joined forces with Native Americans (formerly known as Indians) to try to push Britain out of North America.

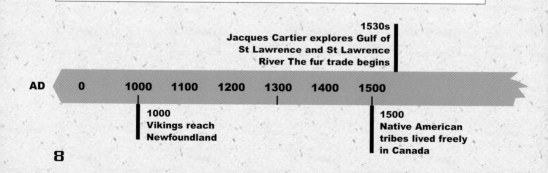

1530s
Jacques Cartier explores Gulf of St Lawrence and St Lawrence River The fur trade begins

AD   0   1000   1100   1200   1300   1400   1500

1000
Vikings reach Newfoundland

1500
Native American tribes lived freely in Canada

8

The French and Indian War ended with Britain's victory and the end of French control of Canada. Many French-speaking people stayed in eastern Canada.

The nation of Canada

Canada was ruled by Great Britain for many years and British control did not formally end until 1982. Canada's history through the 19th and 20th centuries involved adding western provinces to the original eastern settlements. (A province is like a county in the United Kingdom.) The eastern provinces of Nova Scotia, New Brunswick, Québec and Ontario were united by an act of the British Parliament in 1867. New provinces and **territories** – Manitoba, the Northwest Territories, British Columbia, Prince Edward Island and the Yukon – were added in the late 19th century. Saskatchewan and Alberta were added in the early 20th century and Newfoundland was added in 1949.

The process of adding territories continues. The huge northern territory of Nunavut was created in 1999, and is home to much of Canada's Inuit population. Today, Canada is made up of ten provinces and three territories.

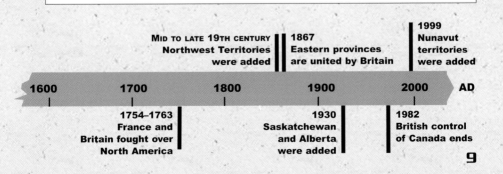

A look at Canada's geography

Canada is a huge country. In fact, Canada is the second-largest country in the world – only Russia is bigger. Canada makes up 40 per cent of the continent of North America.

Land

Canada is a nation of many different landscapes. From east to west Canada stretches across six different **time zones**. Much of Canada lies above the Arctic Circle in the north. Canada's border with the USA stretches for 8895 kilometres (5527 miles) and about 85 per cent of all Canadians live within 300 kilometres (115 miles) of this border.

Tall mountains line Canada in the west and the east. The Canadian Rocky Mountains, or 'the Rockies', in the west are the most famous. More than 50 peaks in the Rockies are higher than 3350 metres. Even taller than the Rockies is the Torngat Range in the east of the country – Canada's tallest mountain range.

A train trip is a one of the best ways to see Canada's many faces. Starting in the east, you will cross lots of waterways and rivers. In the western provinces of Saskatchewan, Manitoba and Alberta, there are flat **plains** similar to the prairie lands of the United States. These flat plains, along with the land of southern Ontario, are important for farming. If you travel to the north, you will find Arctic tundra. Tundra is frozen land which is too cold for many people to live there.

CANADA'S SIZE ▶
Canada covers about
9,976,140 sq km
(3,851,791 sq miles).
Water takes up a
lot of this area –
755,180 sq km
(291,576 sq miles).

▼ Below, Canada is
shown as it appears
on the globe.

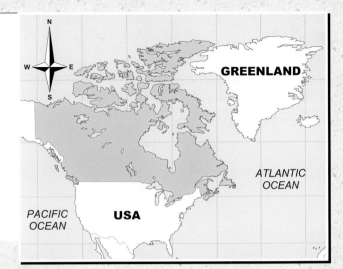

CANADA

★ National capital
● Major city
— River

0   300   600 Kilometres
0   300   600 Miles

Water

Water has played an important part in Canada's history. The first fur trappers to come to Canada from Europe explored the country by boat. Many of Canada's rivers and lakes are connected, which has made it easy for people to travel long distances.

Today, the Gulf of St Lawrence and the St Lawrence River allow ships to travel easily between the east and the midwest. Most ships travel along the St Lawrence Seaway which is like a huge motorway for boats.

In the west, the Mackenzie, Fraser, Columbia, Klondike and Yukon are Canada's great rivers. Hudson Bay and James Bay are the major waterways of the north, but they are less important for trade than those connected to the St Lawrence Seaway.

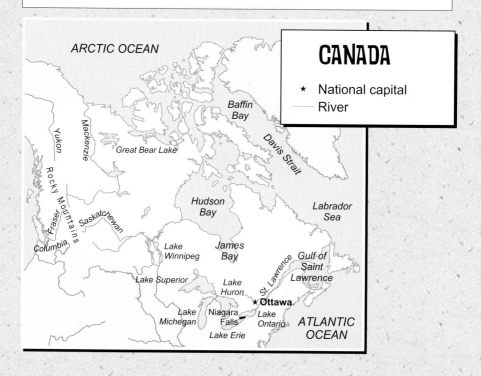

ARCTIC OCEAN

CANADA

★ National capital
— River

Baffin Bay

Davis Strait

Yukon

Mackenzie

Great Bear Lake

Rocky Mountains

Fraser

Saskatchewan

Columbia

Hudson Bay

Labrador Sea

Lake Winnipeg

James Bay

Lake Superior

Lake Huron

St. Lawrence

Gulf of Saint Lawrence

★ Ottawa

Lake Michegan

Niagara Falls

Lake Ontario

ATLANTIC OCEAN

Lake Erie

THE MIGHTY NIAGARA FALLS ▶ Visitors to the Niagara Falls need to wear one of these special yellow raincoats to stay dry. The Falls are very noisy. Niagara Falls is on the border of the province of Ontario and New York State, USA.

◀ **LAKE SUPERIOR** Lake Superior, in Ontario, is one of the five Great Lakes that forms the border between Canada and the USA. The others are Lakes Erie, Huron, Michigan and Ontario.

Weather

Many people think of Canada as a snowy wilderness, but this is not true. Canada has four seasons. In the northern regions, winter can last longer than summer, spring and autumn. Average temperatures in the winter fall below freezing (0°C). During the winter, the ground is usually covered with snow.

In general, the parts of Canada furthest from the ocean are the coldest in winter and the hottest in summer. Ontario and Québec have very hot summers and very cold winters. The northernmost regions have long, cold winters and short, cool summers.

The northern part of Canada is very close to the North Pole, so it is very cold. It is too cold for many people to be able to live there. If you visit northern Canada, you will be able to see icy **glaciers** and Arctic tundra. People who go to this region need special warm clothes and snow boots to protect them from freezing winds and the ice that always covers the ground in to some places.

Rainfall is heaviest in Ontario and Québec. Snowfall is heaviest in the Canadian Rockies and along the Gulf of St Lawrence.

▲ PRINCE EDWARD ISLAND
This is one of the prettiest places to visit in Canada. In summer, you can enjoy warm weather along its beaches. Inland, Prince Edward Island is covered in lush green grass and colourful wildflowers.

CLIMBING IN BRITISH COLUMBIA ▶
Picking a safe path through the ice is a challenge when mountain climbing in winter. These climbers are on Snowpatch Spire on Crescent Glacier in the mountains of British Columbia, Canada's western province.

Toronto: snapshot of a big city

▲ **TORONTO HARBOUR**
Skyscrapers in downtown Toronto are dwarfed by the
CN Tower, the world's tallest building. To its left is the
Skydome arena. There is a great view of the city from the
top of the CN Tower.

Toronto is Canada's largest and most important city. It is not the nation's capital – that is Ottawa – but it is the capital of Ontario, Canada's richest province. Toronto's clean streets and friendly people have led to it being called 'Toronto the Good'.

How Toronto grew

Toronto lies on the north shore of Lake Ontario. This lake forms part of the border between Canada and the USA. Today's city lies on what was once an Iroquois Native American settlement. The Iroquois valued the location because it allowed easy access to land and water **trade routes**. These same routes were later used by explorers, fur traders, soldiers and missionaries.

Today, Toronto still benefits from its location. The St Lawrence Seaway connects Toronto by water with the St Lawrence River, Montréal, Québec and the Atlantic Ocean to the east. Lake Ontario allows Toronto to trade with the US cities south of the Great Lakes, such as Chicago and Detroit.

A modern city

Toronto looks like any modern city. It has many tall buildings, such as the Toronto-Dominion Centre and the Canada Trust Tower. The tallest building in Toronto is the CN Tower. It is actually the tallest building in the world and is 553 metres high. It has become the most recognizable **symbol** of Toronto.

The CN Tower in the heart of Toronto's business district is the perfect place to begin a tour of Toronto. Just a short walk away is the Toronto Stock Exchange. On a weekday, tourists can go in and watch the traders in action. Nearby, 'Mint Corner' is home to Canada's largest banks.

When you have seen where Toronto makes and keeps its money, make your way to the city's beautiful waterfront on Lake Ontario and visit one of the many restaurants along the waterfront's quays. Watch the distant ships on Lake Ontario and the boats close up in its harbour or go on the ferry across to the Toronto Islands.

If you want to do some shopping, then leave the waterfront and head downtown. On Yonge Street you will be able to find every kind of shop you can imagine – clothes, souvenirs, electronics, local crafts – and plenty of restaurants. The St Lawrence Market is a great place to shop for all kinds of food, especially fish and fresh fruit and vegetables.

When you have finished shopping, visit the beautiful St James's Cathedral nearby. It is a wonderful building with a pretty park all around it.

Evening is the perfect time to visit Toronto's Chinatown. It has many unusual shops, art galleries and restaurants where you can try fantastic Chinese food.

TORONTO'S OLDEST RESIDENTS? ▶
The Royal Ontario Museum in Toronto has fascinating exhibits, including prehistoric dinosaur bones.

TORONTO'S TOP-TEN CHECKLIST

If your trip to Canada includes a stop in Toronto, here is a list of ten things you should try to do.

☐ Tour the CN Tower, the tallest building in the world.

☐ Take the ferry to the Toronto Islands.

☐ Watch the busy trading on the floor of the Toronto Stock Exchange.

☐ Shop for cool clothes in the stores on Yonge Street.

☐ Marvel at the high-flying feats of Vince Carter, star of the Toronto Raptors basketball team.

☐ Visit Maple Leaf Gardens, home of one of the original teams in the National Hockey League.

☐ Spend a day shopping and eating in Chinatown.

☐ Enjoy a performance by the Toronto Symphony Orchestra.

☐ Wander the fairgrounds during the annual late-summer Canadian National Exhibition, which features an air show, live theatre and music and much more.

☐ Watch the boats and the day pass by on the Lake Ontario waterfront.

Four top sights

Montréal and Québec

No trip to Canada is complete without a visit to the province of Québec and its two largest cities, Montréal and Québec City. In the province of Québec, people speak French.

Montréal is the largest French-speaking city in Canada, but it is still easy to get around even if you only speak English. Montréal was built on an island in the St Lawrence River. It was originally a centre of Canada's fur trade and also of the Roman Catholic Church in North America.

Mont Royal (Royal Mountain) towers over Montréal and gives the city its name. Montréal is famous for its stylish restaurants and clubs. Young visitors will especially enjoy attractions such as the Biodome. The Biodome has an indoor tropical forest, where you can see tropical animals and plants. There is also a mountain landscape and a polar habitat, where you can see the animals that live in the Arctic parts of Canada. You can also discover what lives in and around the St Lawrence River at the marine ecosystem.

In Québec City, the French influence is even more obvious. Québec is the capital of the province and is Canada's oldest city.

Just outside the city, visit the Plains of Abraham. This is where the French were finally defeated in the French and Indian War. The nearby Laurentian Mountains are a popular site for skiing and other winter sports.

▼ THE CATHEDRAL OF MONTRÉAL

Built between 1870 and 1894, this grand church serves Montréal's large Roman Catholic population.

LIFESTYLES OF THE BIODOME ▶

The Biodome is an environmental museum in Montréal. Inside there are four different ecosystems, or life environments. When it is freezing outside, try a visit to the warm tropical habitat.

Vancouver

Vancouver is a city in the western province of British Columbia. It is called Canada's 'gateway to the Pacific' because it is the centre of Canada's trade with Asia. Tucked between mountains and the Pacific Ocean, it is also one of the most beautiful cities in the world.

While in Vancouver, be sure to look around Gastown, a re-creation of old Vancouver. You can find out how Vancouver looked in the 19th century and what it was like to live there.

Stanley Park covers more than 4 square kilometres (1.5 square miles) near the entrance to Vancouver's stunning harbour. It includes gardens, an **arboretum**, a zoo and a world-famous aquarium. Vancouver is home to a large population of Asian **immigrants**, and is well known for its Chinatown.

Vancouver is ideal for those who love the outdoors. A lot of Vancouver is on the bay, so there is sailing, swimming, and sunbathing on the many beaches. Kayaking and rowing are also very popular. There are many places to rent equipment and even take lessons. Also, you might want to bring some binoculars – the waters around Vancouver provide one of the best places for whale watching.

There are thick forests covering the mountains outside the Vancouver. The nature trails give you a chance to see woodland wildlife.

▲ **FALSE CREEK MARINA**
The marina is the place to moor your boat when sailing into Vancouver, in far western Canada. It is fun to wander among the nearby stores and market before you explore the city.

Its beautiful turquoise (bright blue-green) colour has given Moraine Lake the nickname 'Jewel of the Rockies'.

FASCINATING FACT

The great elk, or Wapiti, can be found high in the Rocky Mountains...or just walking through town. In September, the males gather near Banff National Park. They compete for females by locking antlers. This means they charge at each other, heads down, making a huge crashing sound with their antlers.

The elks sometimes attack cars. They mistake a car for another elk and may try to lock horns with your bumper. If you visit Banff during this time, steer clear of the elks.

Vancouver is one of the most bicycle-friendly cities in the world and many tourists explore the city on rented bicycles. People from Vancouver pride themselves on being athletic and keeping fit. There are often lots of people running in the parks.

The Canadian Rockies

The Canadian Rocky Mountain range is one of the great natural wonders of the world. The Canadian Rockies border the provinces of British Columbia and Alberta and the most spectacular parts are preserved in two national parks, Banff and Jasper.

Banff National Park is in the southern Rockies. It is very popular with tourists. Banff was Canada's first official **wildlife sanctuary** and it is still Canada's most popular resort in both the summer and the winter. One of the highlights of the park is Moraine Lake. Formed by glaciers, Moraine Lake is famous for the bright blue colour of its waters.

Jasper National Park is also beautiful. It is further north and a little wilder than Banff. There are spectacular waterfalls, hot springs and more than 1000 kilometres of walking trails to explore. The Columbia Icefield connects the two parks. It is made up of 30 glaciers that have been there since the last Ice Age.

These National Parks are home to many fascinating animals, including grizzly bears, elks, antelopes, mountain lions, wolves and beavers. Canadians are very proud of their natural heritage.

The Calgary Stampede

Each year in the first and second weeks of July, the city of Calgary in Alberta hosts the Calgary Stampede – the world's biggest **rodeo**. Many call it 'the greatest outdoor show on Earth'.

Calgary is the centre of Canada's cattle-ranching **industry** and the Calgary Stampede celebrates the cowboy's way of life.

The Stampede begins with a huge parade through the centre of Calgary. Each day, there is a rodeo with competitions to demonstrate traditional cowboy skills. These include bronco-busting (riding a wild horse), lasso (or rope) throwing, and steer wrestling. The chuckwagon races are especially popular. You will know when they have started when you see teams of horses pulling wagons around a race track as fast as they can.

At the evenings at the Stampede, you can walk through the Midway, a carnival area, visiting the exhibition halls and stalls where Canada's finest **stock breeders** display their prize cattle and horses. There is an spectacular firework show every night as well as several musical performances.

The special children's area is like a huge amusement park. There are fairground rides and visits by cartoon characters and television personalities and lots of stalls selling souvenirs and hot food.

COWBOYS AT THE CORRAL ▶
These real-life cowboys are checking their schedule for the next event at the Calgary Stampede, 'the greatest outdoor show on Earth'.

▲ CHUCKWAGON RACES
Chuckwagon racing is one of the most exciting events at the Calgary Stampede. Only a skilled driver can keep ahead of the pack – and out of the way of danger.

Going to school in Canada

Each province in Canada has its own way of running its public schools. Québec, for example, tries to preserve its French culture and classes there are taught in French. In the other provinces, classes are taught in English.

Most Canadian children attend one year of kindergarten, eight years of elementary school and four years of high school. The subjects taught are generally the same as in schools in the United Kingdom. Almost all Canadians can read and write.

A large percentage of Canadian students go on to college. Most of Canada's universities are **funded** by the governments of the individual provinces.

▲ GOING TO SCHOOL IN CANADA
These two students are hard at work in a Canadian classroom.

Canadian sports

Canadians enjoy many different sports. There are Major League Baseball teams in Toronto and Montréal and a National Basketball Association team in Toronto. Canada also has a professional American football league, the CFL (Canadian Football League).

Canada's official national game is lacrosse. Players use sticks that have a small net on the top to catch and pass a small, hard ball on an outdoor field. Lacrosse is actually a Native American game which was played long before the Europeans came to Canada.

Ice hockey is one of the most popular sports in Canada. Canadians re-invented hockey as a winter sport and played it on frozen lakes, rivers and ponds. Teams from Canadian cities play in the National Hockey League (NHL). Ice hockey is also very much a small-town sport in Canada. There are hundreds of local sides and many junior leagues.

ICE HOCKEY ▶
Many Canadians take ice hockey very seriously. Thousands pack the stands at local and provincial games to cheer on their favourite teams.

From farming to factories

Canada began as a major **supplier** of fur. Traders shipped furs back to Europe to be used for clothing. Many fur-trading companies became very successful.

The most important parts of Canada's present economy are manufacturing and services. The iron and steel industries are especially important. They produce car parts, mining equipment and household appliances. Canada also **exports** oil and natural gas to countries around the world.

Mining and farming are important, but less than they used to be. Canada produces a lot of the world's grain, especially wheat, but less than 5 per cent of Canadian land can be used for farming.

Nearly 50 per cent of Canada is covered with forests. These forests are used for logging, or cutting down trees, which are used to make wood products.

The fishing industry is largest near Hudson Bay and in the north-west near the Pacific Ocean.

The largest part of the Canadian economy is the service industry. This means that lots of people work in jobs that provide services, such as transport, tourism (especially camping, hunting and fishing), food, recreation, hotels and housing. So some Canadians work as phone operators, bus drivers, cooks or travel agents. Because Canada is so large, transport is especially important, to residents and tourists alike.

LOGGING ▶
Powerful machine jaws help loggers to stack the logs after the trees have been cut down with the aid of huge powered saws. Logging is a very important industry in Canada.

◀ **ON THE ROAD**
Many Canadians love to travel, especially within Canada. Campers and RVs (recreational vehicles) are a popular way to explore this huge country.

The Canadian government

Canada is a parliamentary democracy. It has ten provinces and three territories and each of these is represented in Parliament. Everyone in Canada above the age of eighteen has the right to vote.

Parliament consists of two houses, or parts. The lower house of Parliament is the House of Commons. The upper house is known as the Senate. The governments of the different provinces appoint the Senate's 104 senators.

The head of the government is the prime minister. The prime minister chooses advisers to be members of his or her Cabinet. Although Canada governs itself, the official head of state is the queen or king of the United Kingdom.

CANADA'S NATIONAL FLAG

The Canadian flag, also called the Maple Leaf flag, was adopted in 1964. The red and white colours are the national colours of Canada. Until 1860, the national symbol was the beaver, but in that year the maple leaf became popular and has been the national emblem ever since. Canada is known for its maple trees, which produce wonderful pure maple syrup.

Religions of Canada

People have come to Canada from many different places. and they follow a wide variety of religions. Most, however, are Christian. Just under 46 per cent of Canadians are Roman Catholics. Catholics observe the teachings of Jesus as written in the New Testament of the Bible. The head of the Roman Catholic Church is the Pope, who lives near Rome in Italy. About 36 per cent of Canadians are Protestant. Protestants are also Christians, but have no special leader like the Pope.

Some Canadians are Buddhist, Hindu, Sikh, Jewish or Muslim. More than 1 per cent of Canadians are Jewish. There are very large Jewish communities in both Toronto and Montréal. Muslims, Buddhists, Hindus, Sikhs and followers of Native American religions represent about 3 per cent of the population of Canada.

NOTRE DAME BASILICA ▶
This cathedral in Montréal was completed in 1829.

Canadian food

Canadian food varies greatly depending on where in Canada you are. In Ontario, for example, much of the food you find will be similar to what you find in the United Kingdom or in the USA. In Québec, the food is much more likely to have a French influence.

In cities like Vancouver and Toronto, you will find food from many different cultures, such as Chinese or Korean dishes.

Fish is an important part of the diet in the eastern provinces because of all the fishing that happens in the nearby waters.

A popular Canadian meal is the 'logger's breakfast' which comes from the eastern provinces. A logger's breakfast is pancakes topped with maple syrup with a serving of trempetti (bread soaked in maple syrup and topped with cream) on the side.

◀ MAPLE SYRUP
The sweetness of maple syrup, boiled down from many gallons of sap from the maple tree, was popular with Native Americans in Canada long before the Europeans came. It is so popular that there is even a maple leaf on the Canadian flag.

Canada's recipe

NANAIMO BARS

INGREDIENTS:

FOR THE BOTTOM LAYER:
250 g melted butter
100 g granulated sugar
100 g cocoa
2 eggs
140 g crushed digestive biscuits
100 g flaked coconut
100 g chopped walnuts

FOR THE MIDDLE LAYER:
120 g butter
4 tbsp custard powder
2 drops vanilla essence
3 tbsp of milk
310 g icing sugar

FOR ICING:
225 g plain chocolate
110 g unsweetened chocolate
50 g butter

WARNING:
Always ask an adult to help you cook.

DIRECTIONS:
BOTTOM LAYER: **Mix together the melted butter and sugar. Add the cocoa, then the eggs. Beat until smooth. Add the biscuit crumbs and mix thoroughly. Mix in the coconut and walnuts. Press the mixture into two 22-centimetre square tins. Put in the fridge.**
MIDDLE LAYER: **Cream together the butter, the custard powder and the vanilla. Gradually blend in the milk and icing sugar. Spread evenly over the chocolate base. Chill well before icing.**
ICING: **Melt the chocolate and butter on low heat. Spread on to the chilled middle layer. Chill in the fridge. Cut the cake into bars before the chocolate on top has completely hardened.**

Up close: Nunavut

Nunavut is Canada's newest territory. It was formed by the division of some of Canada's Northwest Territories and it became part of the Canadian **federation** in 1999.

Nunavut measures 1,900,000 square kilometres (733,600 square miles) which is one-fifth of all of Canada's land. Nunavut may be large, but only about 27,000 people live here. Fewer people live in this region than in any other in Canada.

Most of the people who live in Nunavut are Inuit. The Inuit are the native people of northern Canada, Greenland and Alaska. Outside Canada, Inuit are sometimes called Eskimos. However, many people do not like to use the word 'Eskimo' anymore. They prefer the word 'Inuit', which means 'the people' in Inuktitut, the language of the Inuit people.

Nunavut exists because the Inuit people sued the Canadian government for the return of their traditional lands. Non-Inuit people are free to live in Nunavut, but the Inuit govern the territory. The word Nunavut means 'our land'.

Life in Nunavut is very different from life in the rest of Canada. Nunavut is an Arctic region with a harsh, cold climate and spectacular natural beauty. Its landscape includes tundra, lakes, mountain ranges, icebergs and even glaciers. Tundra is a flat, cold area with few trees. Settlements are small and very far apart. Even the capital city, Iqaluit, has a population of only 4500 people.

▲ **BAFFIN ISLAND, IN NUNAVUT**
Icy cold for most of the year, Baffin Island melts
into a beautiful green landscape in the summer.

▼ WHALING

The Inuit people once depended on whale meat to survive.
These Inuit villagers are sharing a bowhead whale. The Inuit
are respectful of the whales and are careful not to take too many.

In most towns, the landing strip for aircraft is their lifeline and link to the rest of Canada.

The 'Nunavut automobile' is a four-wheeled all-terrain vehicle (ATV). An ATV can run on all kinds of ground and in the worst weather. Today's Inuit often ride ATVs to traditional hunting grounds. In winter, which can last from November to April, the snowmobile is the best way to get around because there is so much snow and ice.

The people who live in Nunavut do things like watch television (from satellite dishes), use personal computers and drive snowmobiles, trucks and ATVs. However, many also hunt caribou, seals, walruses, whales, fish and even polar bears. They use the meat and furs to feed and clothe their families. Most Inuit believe that having their own territory gives them the best chance of keeping their culture and customs so that they can last far into the future.

SNOWMOBILES ▶
In many parts of Nunavut a snowmobile is the best way to get around. Ice and snow make the ground too slippery for cars or trucks.

Holidays

Canadian holidays

Canada celebrates several public holidays. Perhaps the most important is Canada Day, which falls on 1 July. On Canada Day people celebrate the day when the Canadian provinces united and became Canada.

Victoria Day is celebrated on the Monday before 25 May. It honours Queen Victoria's birthday. She ruled Great Britain and Ireland from 1837 to 1901.

Canadians celebrate Thanksgiving on the second Monday of October. Canada observes Remembrance Day on 11 November to honour its soldiers killed in the two World Wars and other conflicts. Canada also celebrates Christmas, Easter, New Year's Day and Labour Day (the first Monday in September).

▲ CANADA DAY
Families and friends get together to celebrate being Canadian, with parades, music, good food and fun.

Learning the language

English	French	How to say it
Hello	Bonjour	bon-JHOOR
Goodbye	Au revoir	OH rev-WAHR
How are you	Comment allez-vous?	KOH-mont AH-lay VOO
My name is	Je m'appelle	JHEH mah-PELL
Please	S'il vous plaît	SEE VOO PLAY
Thank you	Merci	mehr-SEE
Excuse me	Excusez-moi	ek-SKOO-say MWAH

SHARE THE ROAD

PARTAGEZ LA ROUTE

Quick facts

Canada

Capital
Ottawa, Ontario

Borders
USA (S, NW)
Greenland (NE)
Pacific Ocean (W)
Atlantic Ocean (E)
Arctic Ocean (N)

Area
9,976,140 sq km
(3,851,791 sq miles)

Population
31,902,268

Main crops and livestock
Wheat, barley, oilseed, tobacco,
fruits, vegetables, forest products,
cattle, fish

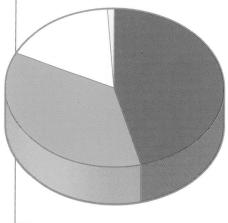

Largest cities
Toronto (4,881,400 people)
Montréal (3,511,800)
Vancouver (2,078,800)
Ottawa (1,107,000)

◄ **Main religious groups**

■ Roman Catholic 46%
▨ Protestant 36%
☐ Other 17%
☐ Jewish 1%

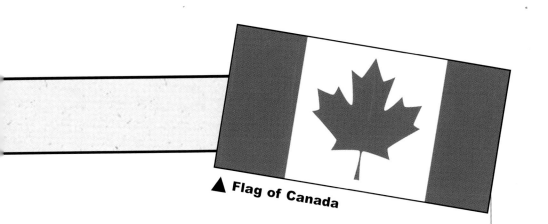

▲ Flag of Canada

Coastline
243,791 km (151,488 miles)

Longest river ▶
Mackenzie
4240 km (2635 miles)

Literacy rate
97% of all Canadians
can read

Major industries
Processed and
unprocessed minerals, food
products, wood and paper
products, transport
equipment, chemicals, fish
products, oil, natural gas

Natural resources
Iron ore, nickel, zinc,
copper, gold, molybdenum,
potash, silver, fish, timber,
wildlife, natural gas,
hydropower, petroleum

◀ Monetary unit
Canadian dollar

People to know

◄ Mike Myers

Mike Myers is just one of several famous Canadian comedians. Born in Scarborough, Ontario, in 1963, his fame began when he joined the cast of the TV programme *Saturday Night Live* in 1989. He branched out into films, which include *Austin Powers* and *Wayne's World*.

Shania Twain ►

Shania Twain was born in 1965 and grew up in Ontario. After losing both parents in a car accident, Twain raised her younger brothers and sister. Twain's music breakthrough came in 1995 with her second album, *Woman in Me*. Her third album, *Come on Over* (1997), has sold more than 34 million copies.

◄ Wayne Gretzky

Ice hockey is Canada's favourite sport, and Wayne Gretzky is the greatest ice hockey player of all time. During his 20-year career, Gretzky set more than 60 National Hockey League records. Gretzky was known for his skill and is loved by Canadians for being a great guy. He retired from ice hockey in 1999.

More to read

Do you want to know more about Canada?
Have a look at the books below.

Continents: North America, M. Fox
    (Heinemann Library, 2002)
Learn about the continent's big cities, countryside and
famous places. Find out about the major landforms,
climate and vegetation, as well as the people and animals
that live there.

See Through History: The Plains Indians,
    Alys Swan-Jackson (Heinemann Library, 1995)
Discover life on the North American Plains, and peel
back four see-through pages to look inside an earth
lodge, a Blackfoot encampment, a ceremonial sweat
lodge and a frontier trading post.

Glossary

arboretum place where special trees are grown

bay crescent-shaped body of water, which can be small or very large

continent one of seven huge land masses on the Earth: Africa, Antarctica, Asia, Australia, Europe, North America and South America

export send to another country for selling purposes

federation group of states that have joined together under one government

founded set up in the beginning

funded gave money to

glacier huge ice mass in the form of a river that is found around the North and South Poles

Ice Age time when the Earth's climate was so much cooler that ice covered most of the continents; there have been several Ice Ages since the Earth formed.

immigrant person who has come from a different country to settle in a new country

industry large business with many people working in different kinds of jobs

missionary person sent out to different regions or countries to tell the people there about their own church's beliefs

plain wide area of land with few trees, usually grassy

rodeo exhibition and contest of cowboy skills

settlement town created by a group of people in a new place

stock breeder person who raises cows, horses, pigs, sheep or other animals in large numbers

supplier someone who gives or sells things that other people need

symbol picture or object that is used to represent something else

territory large division of a country where not many people live

time zone section of the Earth where everybody sets their clocks to the same time

trade route path taken by people on land or sea to bring goods from one country or area to another for sale or trade

wildlife sanctuary place where animals, birds and fish are protected from hunting or destruction

Index